99 Meditations for a Modern-Day Habakkuk

99 Meditations for a Modern-Day Habakkuk

11-9-15

For Alan —
"Because all the easy assignments were gone,
only the hard ones were left."
Many thanks! *Christine Bodine*

CHRISTINE M. BODINE

Published by I*SAY*THANK*YOU*PRESS
Longmont, Colorado 80503

Cover Image: Amanda Robbins, Longmont Colorado
Catching a Blessing, cupped hands in shadow, from Meditation No. 86

Graphic Art Content: Amanda Robbins, Longmont Colorado

Author Photo: Karen Knutsen Quinn Photography, Niwot Colorado

Scripture quotations marked (NIV) are taken from THE HOLY BIBLE, NEW INTERNATIONAL VERSION®, NIV® Copyright © 1973, 1978, 1984, 2011 by Biblica, Inc.® Used by permission. All rights reserved worldwide.

Scripture quotations marked (NLT) are taken from the Holy Bible, New Living Translation, copyright © 1996, 2004, 2007 by Tyndale House Foundation. Used by permission of Tyndale House Publishers, Inc., Carol Stream, Illinois 60188. All rights reserved.

Order from Amazon.com

ISBN 13:9780996470407
ISBN: 0996470409

Library of Congress Control Number: 2015911986
I*SAY*THANK*YOU*PRESS, Longmont, CO
© 2015 I*SAY*THANK*YOU*PRESS

Also by Christine M. Bodine

Souvenirs of Myself

For Ted

Contents

Foreword

DON'T READ THIS book unless you want to be stretched, humbled and encouraged! I've once again been reminded that I'm not alone in my confusion and struggle over the injustices of life.

Christine Bodine writes with unexpected grace, insight and humor. Time and again I chuckled out loud or resonated with deep sighs. It is both beautifully poetic and unexpectedly profound. I'm richer because of it, and I have no doubt that you will be as well.

Oswald Chambers once said, "Doubt is not always a sign that a man is wrong; it may be a sign that he is thinking." I believe that to be true and that Christine has been thinking far more deeply than most. She shines uncommon light on the age old question of why bad things happen to good people.

If you're in need of something more than nice insights, this book will be one that you repeatedly read and treasure as I have, and I'm not alone. A dear family member of ours has faced enormous personal and family challenges resulting in emotional and physical suffering. When she read this little book, she was lifted by the reminder that someone else could relate.

Some mistakenly say, "God will never give us more than we can handle." The truth is that God often allows horrific happenings that are beyond anyone's capacity to handle. The apostle Paul made that clear when he said, "We were crushed and overwhelmed beyond our ability to endure, and we thought we would never live through it. In fact, we expected to die. But as a result, we stopped relying on ourselves and learned to rely only on God, who raises the dead." 2 Corinthians 1:8-9 (NLT).

It's always too soon to give up on God. Ultimately, we must all put our hope in the One who promises to redeem all things.

Dr. Alan Ahlgrim
Founding Pastor
Rocky Mountain Christian Church
Niwot, Colorado

Preface

I AM INEXPLICABLY DRAWN to the minor prophets of the Old Testament—their visions, the futures they saw and shared with us. I am especially drawn to the book of the prophet Habakkuk, a little gem tucked toward the end of the Old Testament, only three chapters long. This is a book you might overlook altogether, given the richness of the Old Testament.

I first discovered Habakkuk in a roundabout way. During a time of trouble, as I often turned to the book of Job, I found myself incredibly jealous of Job's happy ending. Imagine that—I envied Job. When I found myself focused solely on the outcome of Job's story, I knew I should continue searching for a kindred spirit in the Bible with whom I might identify more completely. Certainly, I required a role model who had known trouble, someone who wasn't as righteous as Job. But beyond that, perhaps, I needed a prophet with a distinctive voice, clarity, and wisdom to help me make meaning of this confounding world. And I stumbled upon Habakkuk.

I'm drawn to the prophet because of the way he thinks and sees the world. He questions, he shakes his fist, he does what is necessary to get answers, to be one with his God.

The various Bible commentators have weighed in on Habakkuk. Much of what they have to say is historical, contextual or analytical. For me, however, this has been a spiritual and emotional quest, not an intellectual one. And along the way, I see that I have a kindred spirit in Habakkuk.

Habakkuk struggled for his country's good. Today, the modern-day struggler might focus on unfairness in a world overflowing with conflict and injustice. What is it inside us that tweaks us, that sets us off? It could be the treatment of others continents away. Or it could be close to home. I am mystified as to how we choose our injustices, but perhaps they choose us. It seems to happen very early on in life, and then these injustices never let go. Though we undoubtedly add more to our list when we keep our hearts open.

For me, disease and lack of physical wholeness have always been very great injustices. That one should live inside a human body with greater limitations than that of the next person is a hardship. Some wear this hardship well. Others are restricted or silenced by their limitations.

My understandings of this injustice were sharpened when, as a young mother in my thirties, I volunteered at Marianjoy Rehabilitation Hospital, in Wheaton, Illinois. At Marianjoy, I saw firsthand the devastating effects of brain injury, spinal cord injuries, birth defects, stroke, diseases like diabetes, and many other physical deficits. I learned to round the corner to a hospital room and not stare at the absence of a leg missing beneath the blanket, the grossly crippled fingers, the concave hole in the head. I did not look, but I never forgot the people inside those bodies. Years later, I would become an outpatient at Marianjoy myself due to chronic pain. I began to accept the ways in which I'd tried to outrun fibromyalgia/autoimmune disease because of its frightening nature.

That line we articulate without thinking—if you have your health, you have everything—is best understood on the other side, after you've lost something you're accustomed to having.

Other commonalities we share with the prophet Habakkuk can be understood by scholarly context. In Albert Barnes's Notes on the Bible, the name Habakkuk conjures a beautiful image of God's enfolding the soul:

> The word [Habakkuk] in its intensive form is used both of God's enfolding the soul within His tender support-ing love, and of man clinging and holding fast to divine wisdom. . . . It fits in with the subject of his prophecy, faith, cleaving fast to God amid the perplexities of things seen. Dion.: "He who is spiritually Habakkuk, cleaving fast to God with the arms of love, or enfolding Him after the manner of one holily wrestling, until he is blessed, enlightened, and heard by Him, is the seer here." "Let him who would in such wise fervidly embrace God and plead with Him as a friend, praying earnestly for the deliverance and consolation of himself and others, but who sees not as yet, that his prayer is heard, make the same holy plaint, and appeal to the clemency of the Creator."

The Barnes Commentary offers two possible explanations for the prophet's name, which does not exclude a holy wrestle:

> "He is called 'embrace' either because of his love to the Lord; or because he engages in a contest and strife and (so to speak) wrestling with God." For no one with words so bold ventured to challenge God to a discussion of His justice and to say to Him, "Why, in human affairs and the government of this world is there so great injustice?" *

After years of questioning and wrestling, this collection of meditations came into being. It became the answer, the light of what I longed to know. The meditations are organized into three chapters, just like the book of Habakkuk; they also follow the path of argument, acceptance, and awe, as fist-shaking gives way to listening and understanding. Further, any √

---

* http://biblehub.com/commentaries/barnes/habakkuk/1.htm

meditation inspired by Habakkuk must have a poetic or sublime nature, and so in the meditations I have tried to emulate such a style.

In these New Testament times, our modern-day Habakkuk has a triune God—Father, Son, and Holy Spirit—with whom he or she can supplicate. This forms another arc of the extended meditation here. This triune God becomes more three-dimensional as an authentic relationship forms. By Chapter 2, you will see how Father, Son and Holy Spirit become Creator God, Lord God and Dearest God.

As we would with any complaining two-year-old who wants whatever he or she sees, our heavenly Father ultimately distracts us, tells us to look away from the lack. He says, *Just look over here. This is what I am going to show you today.*

That so many people live on this planet without the vision to simply *look over here* pains me, the same way that all physical lack of capacity pains me. And so I propose a special shout-out to those beautiful people who await visual restoration.

I wish you Godspeed as you pass through the wrestle so that you can linger in the awe.

Longmont, Colorado
June 2015

1

for crying out loud: the argument

How long, Lord, must I call for help,
but you do not listen?

—*Habakkuk 1:2 (NIV)*

1.

Abraham got a case of stars in his eyes.
He believed.

Me, I'm not so much a gazer, grazer,
wanderer. But when I look at the
sky, I'll give you this—I like what
you've done with the place.[†]

[†] *you*—throughout the meditations, unless the context suggests otherwise, the pronoun
you refers to God, generally.

2.

Today, the mountaintops are positively powder white. Hard to say where mountain ends & sky begins.

Did you shake yourself off, blanket the earth with your fury?

Maybe you dusted off your boots before you stepped inside, & you weren't angry at all.

3.

Rail against the machine. We all have to shake & pump a skyward fist occasionally. But you & I have a regular thing—like going out to coffee & giving your friend a scolding—then agreeing to meet the following week. Like a cycle of violence.

I never wanted to be a batterer. It's a real good thing that you're invisible. Otherwise, I'd have to look at the marks I put on you.

4.

I am a child on a great tire swing, on a sturdy branch, on a tall oak tree. You are pushing me not too nicely. I cannot get my bearings. I wobble, I spin. I fear a collision with the tree. But you don't stop.

5.

Another why to the sky.

I demand to know, *Why me? Why must I be afflicted?*

So unladylike of me to shout, yet this is what I am reduced to. I am she-who-is-pretty-exquisite-at-arguing.

I await your response, your legions of soldiers, your cavalry, your impending rescue.

6.

I am in a funk again & running away from you. You, my Creator, are that dangerous hot stove. I touch; therefore, I hurt.

Why shouldn't I attribute my pain to you, if indirectly? You started this world, didn't you? You can't wriggle out of that one.

7.

Why? That my chaff might fly. That's what Gerard Manley Hopkins wrote concerning his gain from personal crisis.

What if I don't want my grain to lie sheer & clear? What if I don't care?

8.

Ready to rumble. Welterweight champ, right here. I fight; therefore, I am. You are my toughest opponent. I fight, yet I am destined to lose.

9.

After many wandering decades in your world, I'm not sure I've found what
I'm looking for—what should I have acquired?

    You say, *On-the-job training, big heart, soft skills.*

    I say, *What more can I know, as sun wanes & moon grows?*

    You say, *Here is readiness for what's to come.*

    I say, *Can't I live exquisitely, here & now?*

10.

The hour after the hour I first believed, I prayed you would bring me through the trial, & I would emerge on the other side. Years later, I wonder if that's fantastical thinking.

Am I bound for a better, distant shore? Am I sentenced to wander the desert without exit?

Do you plan to leave me right where you found me?

11.

The birds at my window this morning—was that you? Did you send an offering of chattering sparrows? Next time we patch things up between us, I want you to know: I'm a flower girl.

12.

I didn't tell you go away. I said go easy on me. Go mercy on me, my earthly song, by the shores of great mercy, full-court-press mercy.

Please say you are—another sleepless night of begging & longing.

13.

Long-suffering Job. Yeah, that's the fate I wanted (not). I have considered your servant Job more than I care to admit. I struggle to grasp your intentions— why make such a spectacle out of one man? If I were in your celestial shoes, I'd spread the misery around.

(nota bene to the reader: to be clear, I did not observe God's celestial shoes.)

14.

Listening ears. I have one more favor to ask of you. Please hear me now so I won't have to cry out any longer—

I am so over this earthly journey thing. What I wouldn't give for just a slip of heaven while on earth.

15.

Cinderella, glass slipper, broken pieces. Cut my foot. Badly bleeding.

16.

I completely understand John Keats & his cave of quietude—*there anguish does not sting; nor pleasure pall.* Pure survival mode.

    & furthermore—*the man is yet to come/ Who hath not journeyed in this native hell.*

    Seen it, been there, done that. When they gave out Girl Scout badges for this cave, I earned mine many times over. I remember what they told me that day I received the badge—

    Here is the Cave of Quietude badge, awarded to those who are exceptional at stoic living.

    Onto the next badge. I pray it won't require courage.

17.

Today I beg of you—do not listen to me if I tell you I don't care. Please do not believe me. I am too small to say such things. I am like Lara in *Doctor Zhivago*—at the train station, don't let go of my hand.

18.

I found out this morning that I'm alive for one more day. For that, I give you wake-up thanks. You are the one who will hear my prayer. Another daily dose of earth, to live on the cusp of what breath you give. In exchange, I offer petitions, fits, doubts, reflections. Hardly seems right.

19.

About the other day—I didn't say you weren't real. Please don't put twisted thoughts in this head. Don't think of leaving me, either. Without you, whom would I wrestle with?

20.

It's your world, & a pretty unjust one at that. Do what you like with it. But then, you can't say I can't complain. We've been over this topic before, haven't we?

21.

Every now & then, we have to give a dog a bone. Today is that day. Please give me mine now.

22.

We cannot keep secrets between us. Trust me when I say I pour it all onto the page, for you. I hold nothing back. If I've thought it, I've said it. You already know, you know-it-all.

23.

Why do I talk so much? All yammer & jawbone, that's me. Perhaps I'm afraid if I stop talking, you'll forget about me. So on & on I go.

& you—strong, silent type—macho quiet, cool customer. Is this your version of the silent treatment? Like a man of great mystery, you reel me in.

24.

You taught me to hold loosely the things I love. Be prepared, to release my grasp. Ready at a moment's notice. Like a minuteman, if necessary, I come to your side, my life, as you wish.

Till that day, I am talkback & toil.

25.

Like that time at the Chicago train station, when I lost my favorite umbrella. I went down to the bowels of the building, believing in good Samaritans, rang that silly little bell, summoned the old man behind the counter, chancing he would produce it, he would have it, yes, right behind his counter. But he didn't have my umbrella.

Is there any chance you're running a lost & found repository? & what qualities-capacities-health we've lost throughout our lives can yet be collected?

I had to ask. Because I wonder where you're putting all those things you've taken from us.

26.

Wrestling—is that akin to restless? I rummage through racks at the Goodwill store, yet nothing here to buy, nothing I desire. Artifacts that other people recycled, as if to say, *this silk plant didn't work out for me, after all, it didn't hold the answer.* While we're at it, what is the question?

Self-help books, the stained bath towel, chipped vase, slight sundress, board games with missing pieces—no keepers here.

27.

I am she-who-has-lost-health-wealth-family (fill in the blank)—like water, life's treasures slipped through my hands.

    Why do you put up with rants-of-persistent-woman? One day, you'll tell me what you got out of this. Till then, I will try to be polite & just say thank you.

28.

Surely you heard it——that guttural, almost inhuman cry. Pain lodged so deep, I could not believe the sound came from me.

I must protest these living conditions, this squalor of the soul.

I hurt. All of your people hurt.

Now that I've gotten that scream out of the way, could you hurry up, please? Come take care of us.

29.

Last night, I saw a translucent blue bottle atop my dresser. Its label read—
Acquiescence perfume
Bend, bow and bop to the will of God
Come get faith
I woke up before I could put on the perfume, & the bottle was gone.

30.

On a good day, we are jewels of the beloved. I am diamond, ruby, sapphire. How to live like that?

You went to the trouble to make me beautiful. But sometimes, I feel like a chip of broken glass. Washed up like litter on the seashore—overlooked, left behind, a danger to bare feet.

2

gliding above the rubble: the acceptance

I will climb up to my watchtower
and stand at my guardpost.
There I will wait to see what the LORD says
and how he will answer my complaint.

—*HABAKKUK 2:1 (NLT)*

31.

Last night, I swear I heard a voice whisper to me, *Holy Trinity Fancy Pants.* Such a confounding phrase, enough to wake anyone with a startle.

Now you've got my attention. I must get to the bottom of this. I must find out who wears these fancy pants.

32.

Strange how I talk one minute to you, Father; then you, Son; then you, Spirit. As if you are triplets, I interchange & confuse your identities.

Please don't take offense at my faux pas. Mea culpa. I want to be friends with all three of you.

Creator God, I know you well enough to kvetch. What more?

My Lord God, you were a presence. You arrived in an earthly wrapper. They say when you passed by, it was a beautiful thing—first, the rustle of your garment, then, that supernatural brush with the divine.

To the elusive Spirit, I will give you a new name. Something that says whom I need you to be, so you'll know it's me calling. I will name you Dearest God, which means . . . noble & worthy.

33.

Today, I swear I heard you say, *Come to the desert. I will end your years of aimless wandering. There, all will be made clear.*

You beckoned me come at sunrise, when the world is new. No one around. Have the house to myself.

At first morn, it's all about the light, isn't it? The way it slants & creeps across the rocks. These illuminated red cliffs, like tinker toys you arranged for my amusement — a pillbox sits atop that far mountain, or maybe it's a crusty sandwich.

It's the high relief of the thing, that something's-bigger-than-me thing. You knew what you were doing. Perhaps you had prior experience at this creation business. Isn't this desert everything you wanted it to be? I remove my hat, observe the silence.

In this harsh land, I am too much at peace. Holy, dusty ground, crushed stone of my rebirth. I surrender.

34.

The high desert is quiet today. No one to distract me on this early morning walk. A stray lizard darts by. The scent of pine fills the air. Purple & yellow wildflowers, tempting to pick, arrange themselves along the road.

Instead, I leave them behind for those who follow. *Please look after them for me.* I must travel light. My stay here is temporary, I know, I know.

35.

At these altitudes, I can tell you're fond of peaks & plateaus—plentiful as far as eye can see. Slickrocks like loaves of dough waiting for yeast to rise, ready to heave & lift higher, as if they aren't done growing yet. Creation still groans, just like me.

Which ones are your top rocks? Show me what you've got. Which ledge did you love best? Tell me.

36.

Creator God, where you split the earth to fasten a river, we call that a canyon. I must observe this phenomenon for myself. Peer down inside. Examine the identity (or lack of) the place.

I travel long & far to arrive at the first overlook. Something about the concavity of the scene touches me—that hollowness, an absence, a kindred spirit—call it what you will.

Oh canyon, my canyon—your erosion hasn't fazed you in the least. You've accepted your aging lot. You've been chipped away, windblown & washed up, bit by bit. Yet you carry on despite your shallow state. Bravo. Well done.

37.

Dearest God, if you've ever loved me, show me. Show me you care about the details of my life. If the hairs on my head matter, take away my fear of the future, fear of the unknown.

It's just you & me against this world—sometimes it's ugly & mean. It's pretty raw down here, wouldn't you agree?

I'm a woman with no one to look after her. I'm troubled & I need a healing. I ask you—be my protector, be my provider. This is my prayer. I think I'll end it now. Amen.

38.

I don't know how they came up with that word *fasting*. It should be *slowing*, for this is how we move about when we're hungry.

Today, I'm fasting & it's about rest, isn't it? That's what fasting requires of me.

& in this slowed state, you'll meet me, won't you? You'll be present in the water I drink, the air I breathe. In place of food, I take you in.

39.

Creator God, I wonder why you enabled a world with illness. Was it so that we couldn't feel proud forever?

Was it a scheme to help us let go our grasp of the world? As John Keats once observed, *Therefore, on every morrow, are we wreathing / A flowery band to bind us to the earth.*

What were you thinking when disease first appeared?

If you're fishing for compliments on this one, let me tell you, I'm not a fan.

40.

My lady, the sky—she can't make up her mind this morning. Will she be cloudy or clear? What will she wear?

Whatever color goes well with blue. Perhaps searing pink, etched with yellow, drama sure to catch a sailor's eye.

Now she has my attention. I can't look away from her brilliance. How I wish I had a blue-sky life, too.

41.

Every now & then, I pat my heart, as if to say, *there, there.*

42.

Just like Moses, I long for rest in Midian.[‡] Time & space between deserts.
Respite. That place where you hand me back my life—no—a better life
than the one I lost.

   Let me live in the stone house near the well. Let there be heaps of food,
laughter, friends around an endless table, cups held up to the sky. Let the
crops be fierce. Let there be no wants, for a while.

   Before I slip on my sandals & you send me off on my journey.

[‡]   An ancient region of northwest Arabia east of the Gulf of Aqaba.

43.

Either you made a mistake & blurred the seasons. Or maybe you just outdid yourself. I'm referring to this morning's snowfall—so delicate, so intricate, like wisps of milkweed taking to a chilly spring sky.

As with so much in the world of art, the line between mistake & genius, not so clear.

Just for today, Creator God, I'll give you all the credit. Milkweed snow—I like it. I like where you're going with this creation theme.

44.

This ritual where I bang my knees to wood for you has grown old like me. Maybe you thought that giving me strength to endure was enough. I'm here to tell you, no, it's not enough. My heart wants something more—& what that something is, I cannot say.

45.

I carried out the death of the daisies today. I attacked their patch of earth. They'll be no more. & I've got cut daisies to bring to their funeral.

46.

Today, I woke up full of fear. So here it is, I'll tell you—I'm afraid if I pray too hard, you'll send me another trial instead. Because your world has given me more than a cupful of disappointment.

If my fears are founded, if you can't heal me this time, pass over me. I need grace, or I'll take a bye.

47.

From the warm glance of the morning sun, I do believe you're smiling, you're still thinking this creation gig was a good idea. Not perfect, perhaps (because of man & woman), but very good.

    & as for me, I don't want to let you down, Creator God.

    Maybe I'll create. Maybe I'll finger paint—because you're a hands-on artist, & I want to be like you.

48.

Today, I pray to know your quiet-spirit-tremble. I need more unseen glimpses of you, Dearest God.

   As you rise & fall inside my chest with each breath & heartbeat——me & you. Invisible version of God-with-me——I pray you, *Stay awhile.*

49.

The wind you sent to visit me this morning—I must report that it behaved in a boastful way.

When it first arrived, the wind told me: *I can make this pretty garden better. I may not be music, but watch me make these flowers dance.*

Then the wind issued great gusts. The tulips shimmied & shook. & before long, I joined them—your wind gave me the shimmies. Your wind made me dance, too.

(nota bene to Creator God: about the boasting, never mind.)

50.

Let's suppose you could only heal my body or my heart. *Pick one*, you say. *Which one will it be?*

    If you can only heal one, make it my heart. Don't let me exit this world bitter & battered. Don't let me be that person. O please.

51.

Please don't let me grow too indifferent to rise up before dawn for the Perseids.[§]

As I rest on the hood of my car, I watch & wait for streaks of meteoric light to fall from the sky—*catch a falling star & put it in your pocket. . . .*

Nature's fireworks pop & glisten. Nothing to show for a while & then, an illuminated arc sprawls across the night— *save it for a rainy day.*

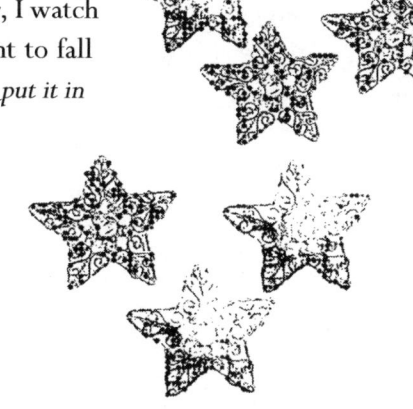

[§] A prolific group, or shower, of meteors associated with the comet Swift-Tuttle that appears annually about August 11.

I look up in stillness; observe the downturned mixing bowl that is our sky. In time, a light blue tincture creeps into view from the east. I know what this is—how I long to shush it, to delay its entrance. Another bold flash catches my eye. I am rewarded for my early morning foray.

Now the slip & crawl of light from the east comes from our impatient sun. Growing luminescence exposes more details—airbrushed clouds emerge & dangle, their pink underbellies exquisite, brilliant.

Another time there will be sky-high streaks. I let the beauty of day break open the cave of my heart.

52.

When I was small, one more was important: one more scoop of ice cream, one more minute catching fire flies in the summer night, one more present under the Christmas tree. Even after I got my way, I wondered, *is that all there is?*

Now that I am older, I can foresee asking for one more year, one more chance to see my son.

Someday, the one more litany ends, when this earth has nothing left to give me. Then, it's day one of eternity with you—Creator, Lord, Dearest. I am woman-on-the-path-to-coming-home.

53.

Last night, I saw myself embark on the Forgiveness Road Trip. Kind of like a rock star concert tour—see the USA, see my past in a new light.

I traveled around the country, sought out friends & family, asked their forgiveness. Mostly, they granted me forbearance. I fed off their grace, pressed on.

I had rented a large RV for the occasion, began the trip in New Jersey, went down to Maryland, south to Florida, back up to Pennsylvania, Ohio, Indiana, Illinois & Iowa. Even swung down to Arizona. Then, back home to Colorado. I rested. & it was very good.

54.

This morning, the ballerina led yoga class. & with all the grace of her glory days, she began with feet in second position. She extended her arms overhead. We extended our arms overhead. She pliéd. We pliéd.

We graying wonders followed our instructor with much less aplomb—we the broken, we the misshapen, we of the bad hips & knees club.

Yet through your lens, Dearest God, I saw nothing but beauty—& I saw each of us the way we might have been, the way we could have been, once upon a time.

55.

Last night, I was a tiny dancer. I saw myself lifted high on the shoulders of my dance partner. & that's how I made it through the trouble—I glided above the rubble.

56.

I'd like to report on the little boy you asked me to look after—he runs to me. There, in the classroom, when he sees me in the doorway, he comes. & though he is another mother's child, my heart opens to him. I find it impossible to dwell on troubles when I make Play-Doh cookies with a little boy like him.

57.

I went to Rabbit Mountain this morning, where your wind pursued me, teased my hair & tumbled the weeds. As I searched for prickly pear cactus flowers, before long, something else happened, something much bigger, maybe even God-size, you could say. & I was a witness to it—the wind took my chaff & I saw it fly away.

58.

These past days, the floodwaters came to town, yet you spared me from the St. Vrain's fury. My very own Passover—trouble all around, but as for me & mine, nothing was touched.

I do not understand why. An uncommon grace. & from this day forward, I will search diligently till I find a reason for this favor.

(nota bene to Creator God: if this is the Passover I prayed for, at midnight, let the North Star wink once for yes, twice for no.)

59.

Every now & then I feel fear & slippage, like I'm going under. You taught me that I have flowers & stars & desert going for me. I've got you & you & you pulling for me, lifting me out of muck & mire.

To you mighty threesome: I pray you, *Lift me above the quicksand of these circumstances. Don't let go of me.*

60.

Dearest God, why do I still argue with you? Is it so that we can make up?

If you & I were married, we would have been off to couples counseling by now. On the sofa, I would explain to our counselor that for once, I long to have the final word between us. I would point to the unequal bargaining power in this relationship. How lopsided, how unfair it is.

Perhaps our counselor would agree with me. She might even declare us incompatible & our differences, irreconcilable.

But for the fact that you will never leave me. You are commitment. You are perfect love.

61.

Creator God, I wonder how you invented dirt. You referred to dry ground as land, but really, it's just dirt.

    I guess life's not always pretty, is it? & yet green growing things come from such ugliness. Here is a substance I avoid, yet need. Beauty out of ugly—how'd you think that up? Pure genius.

62.

I search my garden for the last rose of summer, though I won't know till hindsight which one it was.

Thus I am compelled to treasure each late bloomer—inside my cupped hands, a soft peach fragrant sphere—could this be the last?

63.

When I do not know how to pray, you, Dearest God, groan for me.

Though today, you put new words to my lips. A holy cacophony, a litany, a chant, a prayer language—no matter the name.

Today, I beseech you, mighty threesome, not knowing what I say, or what I pray for:

Oh, A-ra-ma
Oh, A-ma-na
Oh, A-pa-pa
Oh, A-bah-ja
Oh, A-ma-na
Oh, Da-ba-na
Oh, A-pah-tah
Oh, A-ma-na-na
Oh, A-pah-tah-tah

Oh, Ab-sha-nan
Oh, A-la-ba
Oh, Ha-ma-na
Oh, Ar-a-ma
Ohhh Ahhh

3

another pilgrim's progress: the awe

Lord, I have heard of your fame;
I stand in awe of your deeds, Lord.

—Habakkuk 3:2 (NIV)

64.

Last night, in the clearing, some bright meadow, I saw myself at play. You three gentle giants held hands. I was safe in your midst.

As you skipped in a circle, I twirled about. My dizzy fingertips nearly perceived a brush of cloak. & then I knew——you three are here & now.

I pray you every child's prayer: *Play with me awhile, could you?*

65.

On a good day, I rush to your mountain, sing to the wind. But some days, happiness isn't there, as if a pickpocket pinched it from me.

I've struggled against the wrong opponent, haven't I?

Oh, the mirage of this world—these past years, I thought I was taking on friendly fire. Turns out, there was a real enemy after all.

66.

Last night, I saw myself standing waist-high in a field of daisies, their yellow &
white selves glistened in the moonlight. I picked a tall daisy & plucked off its
petals, one at a time, saying:

forgive you
forgive you not
forgive you
forgive you not
forgive you
forgive you
forgive you
& before long, the flower stalk was clean, for a greater purpose—so
that I could be clean, too.

67.

As I climb Eagle Wind Trail at Rabbit Mountain, I collect wildflowers on the way up, one for each buttonhole in my jacket. Behind me, the red & gold of autumn's last breath. From here, the days grow shorter & darker.

The downhill trek requires all my attention—left foot, right foot, left, then right. I select the best rocks to step on, avoiding the loose ones in my quest for terra firma, & before long, my left-right hiking cadence begins to sound like *swing your partner, do-si-do.* The grasshoppers get in on the action, leapfrogging just ahead of me. & somewhere on this rocky trail—me, with my floppy, flower buttons, singing a down-the-mountain square dance tune—I remember what this is. It's called joy.

68.

Like that nursery rhyme—
How many miles to Babylon?
Three score miles and ten.
Can I get there by candle-light?
Yes, & back again.
If your heels are nimble & light,
You may get there by candle-light.

Years have passed. I've seen Babylon. & I left it some time ago. In the distance—
who knows when?—comes the faint glow of home.

69.

Every now & then, we have to let go of something—clean the clutter, ditch a bad habit or two, ditto that for my sins. I wouldn't mind shaking off this journey debris, then, resting a bit.

Unless you have other plans, of course. I pray you, *Tell me*.

70.

Last night, I drove a sports car down the fast lane of I-25—silver convertible with a stick shift—when suddenly, a metal visor slammed down over the windshield, obstructing my view. Instant loss of visibility. Pure darkness, as if in a cave.

Mid-traffic, I applied the brakes. This pilgrim with a fast car wasn't going anywhere.

71.

Last night—pursuers, demons. Images that shook me, woke me with a whimper, outsized fears, stuff of the netherworld.

I pray you, *Repair my faulty night vision. Replace it with a hopeful hue. Something pretty, perhaps paisley pink.*

(nota bene to Creator God: Or you could just surprise me. Which is what you usually do anyway.)

72.

Today, in your sanctuary, Miss Viv reaches for my hand, then squeezes it in that universal language of pilgrims. Her touch tells me, *I know, I know.* As long as I live, I will never tire of linked hands.

Our Father who art everywhere——in heaven, on earth & most especially next to me in the flesh of your creation.

Some of my favorite sisters have gone back to you too soon. I wasn't ready to part with them. Years past, I'd have called you that taunt reserved for people who take back their gifts.

Now, I see how you fill my days with slant versions of my gone-away friends. I walk & move among new breathing beauties——these who assuage my pain, these who pray me back into the ranks of the living.

73.

Creator God, I wonder how you invented color. My eyes so readily accept a wide range of hues—striations of yourself, no doubt. You must be one decked-out-amazing-rainbow-colored dude.

Yet it didn't have to be this way. We could be resigned to a black & white world, if that's what you wanted.

For those without sight, you'll have a special show waiting on the other side. You'll catch them up real good, won't you?

(nota bene: It's you, Creator God, isn't it? You are the one with the fancy pants, aren't you?)

74.

I say, *What happens to my enemies in heaven?*

You say, *That's all over. They'll have nothing but love for you. As if they can't even remember what the disagreement was all about.*

75.

Months pass. More time spent with my invisible friends.

Creator God, yesterday you took me to a plateau where we observed the brown, furrowed rows of a spring planting below. Recumbent possibilities. Lines resting so impossibly straight, like shoots of bamboo laid in a row, one to the next. A harvest in waiting.

You said to me, *This next leg of the journey requires a certain lightness, a buoyancy. Like tilled soil.*

Hmmm, what to make of that? I'm still thinking about what you said. Some days, I am a very slow thinker.

76.

You say, *One day, you may see that yearning after physical capacity is a false love.*
I say, *Forgive me, my Creator, for I only want what I had before.*
You say, *I will do something in your day that you will not believe.*
I say, *Show me your marvels.*

77.

Last night, you three—a mighty threesome—huddled over my beating heart, actively engaged in its repair.

As I recall, Creator God, you plunged your hands into my chest. No drugs, no knives. As you kneaded my heart muscle, you reassured me, *I won't hurt you one bit.*

As always, you were right.

Then you, my Lord & Dearest, joined in the shaping & pressing till I felt the warmth of your healing conspiracy.

78.

Today, I swear I heard you say, *If you love me, love my people. If you love this world, bring something to it.*

What shall I bring, my Lord? Help me leave something of myself behind—because you're a giver. & I want to be like you.

79.

Last night, I called out, *Where are you, oh shy Dearest?*

    I swear I heard you say, *I am that God who danced with you on the train hill many years ago. When the grasses swayed & you swooned, I was there. I am he-who-comes-when-summoned.*

    Do not leave me, then, I said. *I am she-who-summons-you-minute-by-minute.*

80.

Last night, Creator God, you & I sat at the edge of a boat dock beside a vast lake. We dangled our legs & pondered the sky. You showed me some of your favorite stars. You explained to me why you put them where they appear. *There's Arcturus,* you said, pointing out a flicker just past the Big Dipper handle. *If you look to the left, maybe you can see Vega, too.*

Suddenly, our conversation shifted. You said something about making a gift to me. I couldn't quite hear what you said.

Nevertheless, I responded hastily. *I'm not sure you can give away the stars twice. Didn't you already promise them to someone?*

Now that I am awake, I won't question you. One way or another, there will be stars for me.

81.

Last night, Lord God, you & I went off on a rock hunt, in search of geodes to add to my collection. You knew of a place we could look. So we traveled to a vast open space with limestone features.

As we hiked a craggy trail, you thought it would be great fun to lift up the ordinary rocks trapped in hardened earth. So we tugged & turned over several wedged ones to observe what was underneath. We noticed how the ground retained a beautiful imprint, rather like a mold, when each rock was first freed. Sometimes, we found a creeping creature.

I watched you closely, admired your laughter & delight. You & me, Lord God, on an expedition together. I am she-who-lifts-her-face-toward-the-sun. & you, son of the ultimate scientist.

82.

Last night, I was desirous to find lichen & grasses. Just a snippet of Great Basin wild rye, sedge, beargrass. There's nothing like wispy growing things to round out a girl's spring color collection.

    My Lord God, you came along. You are my God who hikes beside me, who climbs, who goes before me.

83.

Creator God, I swear I heard you say, *The wildflowers at alpine level are exquisite in July. Go. See. Touch, feel, smell. Inhale the beauty & you will be rewarded.*
  Take my Son with you, my dear flower child. He knows the way.

84.

We take up our walking sticks & we walk. We take plenty of water. I know not the way, but I have you, my Lord.

Find something to admire each day, you call out to me over your shoulder. *If you cannot find ocean, find lake, find river. If you cannot touch the water, listen to it. Do not be denied the joy of discovery.*

85.

I see your feet, my Lord, just ahead of me. You navigate the narrow trail. I do not look up, though I realize a nearly impossible incline lies just ahead. I look at your feet. I follow your every move. We never run out of mountain.

Spread out on either side of us, an array of Townsendia, coneflower, Rudbeckia.

I see your feet. I follow.

Alpine sunflower, salsify, pussytoes.

Ever higher we climb. The wind grows & blows. I see your feet. We never run out of mountain.

86.

Above bristlecone pine, above tree line, above barren land & tundra lies a
desolation of sorts. We climb to that very pinnacle. I shiver from the cold,
but I draw close to you, my Lord. You share your wrap with me.

Look down, you tell me. *Look at the view below.*

I am at the top of the world with my Lord God. You are
he-who-enables-me-to-tread-the-heights.

I realize my hands are wide-open, my palms expectant of a blessing—
I could catch one right now, should it tumble to earth.

87.

Set before us now——a light dusting of clouds. Enough for me to believe that earth can touch the sky, if it stands on tiptoes. & as dusk approaches, very soon these mountains could reach up to fasten a star or two.

We pause to rest halfway down. We sprawl out on this fancy earth your Father crafted by hand. We feast. We inhale the quiet.

That's when I knew, *the Lord is in his holy temple, the earth is silent before him.*

Our time of rest passes too quickly.

Let us go back down, you say.

I am no longer restless, but ever so reluctant to go.

88.

Last night, Creator God, you presented me with an exquisite pair of glasses, in honor of a successful climb. You told me, *This is the way to better sight.*

When I put on the glasses, I observed your world with spectacular definition, as if for the first time. As if someone washed the windows to my eyes.

I saw your creation, your panoply, how incredible it is.

If I had a hammer & a chisel & one hundred years, I couldn't create one remnant of what you have commanded into existence before me.

Then, I discovered your glasses worked in reverse. I could look deep into myself, as if for the first time, as if someone had washed the aperture to my soul.

(nota bene to Creator God: thank you for tending to my night vision troubles.)

89.

When was the last time you explored a prairie? you ask.
I don't know, my Creator, I confess. *It's been some time.*
Go. Look for wild indigo, compass plant, blazing star. Take my Son, he knows the way.
We make the journey—me, my Lord & my exquisite glasses.
& as before, I am rewarded.

90.

I beg you, Lord, I say. Come with me to the ocean. Let me see this place through you & with you.

You express your delight. You say, *Few sights are more thrilling than successive waves, the way each one breaks & foams at the edge of the sand. It is a place of astounding energy.*

We arrive at the coast to find creatures of the oldest & oddest kind crawling about. The loudness of the wave rhythm comforts me—unexpectedly, strangely.

When we look to the horizon, blue sky meets blue sea. Such persistence, this blue on blue.

Sand & seashells at our feet—so heartbreakingly beautiful. Yet these trinkets mean nothing when I consider how you saved me once, my Lord. Now you've come back to save me twice.

91.

Cumulus clouds angle above me—so still—constructed like an upper room overlooking the main floor of our two-story universe. You've got to love those vaulted ceilings.

& at daybreak, the added appearance of a pink gleam, as if someone left the light on upstairs. One of us may have to flick off the switch. & since you're closer, I say it's you.

I can't help but look up when you distract me like this, my Creator. & wasn't that the whole point of this exercise?

I'll bet you three are laughing to yourselves, *Got you! Made you look!*

You've turned me into a gazer. I am she-who-beholds-creation-with-wonder-&-delight.

92.

I say, *If the clouds could arrange themselves into a message for me, what would you
have them tell me, my Creator?*
　　You say, *W O R T H Y . . .*

93.

Last evening, my Lord, you came to me most solemnly as I was putting the day to bed. You said, *The purpose you have prayed for & longed for is now. I did not lift you up off your knees, then give you nothing to do.*

As I drifted off to sleep, I thought, *This is the answer. On my way toward the life that is truly life.*

94.

Today, I visit the little boy you asked me to look after. He is fascinated with stickers & he always wants to earn one whenever I come to school.

I ask him, *Do you want to make some stars, just like these stickers?*

He nods.

So we practice with a marker on the white board. I explain my two methods. *You can either make two triangles on top of each other, one pointing up & one pointing down, just like this. Or, you can take your marker & make five lines without lifting the point—like this—one, two, three, four, five.*

He tries both ways. Over & over we practice until a galaxy of stars appears before our eyes.

95.

I will plant a fig tree, a grapevine, an olive tree. A fig tree for my Creator, who makes all things fancy. A grapevine for my Lord, who travels great lengths to give me purpose. An olive tree for my Dearest God, the best invisible friend a girl could ever have.

96.

The things I've thought & said, Dearest God, in my anger, I regret. What's done is done.

    If I could make it up to you. I could testify to your power & to your life. Because you're a soother & a healer & a helper & a friend. & don't you know how much I longed for you? & I want to be like you.

97.

Last night, my Lord, you & I climbed the Tree of Life—its trunk & branches so vast & tall. I stayed close so I wouldn't lose sight of you. We had our fill of adventure, & then we rested under the Tree of Knowledge. When we read out loud together, you breathed life into every scripture & I began to see the grand scheme, & I do believe I saw your Father smiling at us.

98.

Creator God, you put a veil of protection over me. So real, I could feel its lacy texture. A reminder that you are here. & after too many years of independent thinking, I must have you. & my Lord God. & my Dearest God. All three.

99.

Last night, my Lord, you & I traveled a winding road. On our way, we encountered a massive stone wall, more massive perhaps than those of Jericho. It was skyscraper tall. I hesitated. Had you not been by my side, I would have gone back immediately.

You saw my concern & said to me, *I will turn this wall into a doorway.*

As soon as you spoke the words, a doorway appeared.

I knew we would go through that doorway. But as it turns out, not today.

Appendix 1: Book of Habakkuk

Habakkuk 1 New Living Translation (NLT)[**]

1 This is the message that the prophet Habakkuk received in a vision.

Habakkuk's Complaint

2 How long, O Lord, must I call for help?
    But you do not listen!
"Violence is everywhere!" I cry,
    but you do not come to save.
3 Must I forever see these evil deeds?
    Why must I watch all this misery?

[**] https://www.biblegateway.com/passage/?search=Habakkuk+1-3&version=NLT

Wherever I look,
> I see destruction and violence.
I am surrounded by people
> who love to argue and fight.
4 The law has become paralyzed,
> and there is no justice in the courts.
The wicked far outnumber the righteous,
> so that justice has become perverted.

The Lord's Reply
5 The Lord replied,
"Look around at the nations;
> look and be amazed!
For I am doing something in your own day,
> something you wouldn't believe
> even if someone told you about it.
6 I am raising up the Babylonians,
> a cruel and violent people.
They will march across the world
> and conquer other lands.
7 They are notorious for their cruelty

and do whatever they like.
8 Their horses are swifter than cheetahs
    and fiercer than wolves at dusk.
Their charioteers charge from far away.
    Like eagles, they swoop down to devour their prey.
9 "On they come, all bent on violence.
    Their hordes advance like a desert wind,
    sweeping captives ahead of them like sand.
10 They scoff at kings and princes
    and scorn all their fortresses.
They simply pile ramps of earth
    against their walls and capture them!
11 They sweep past like the wind
    and are gone.
But they are deeply guilty,
    for their own strength is their god."

Habakkuk's Second Complaint
12 O Lord my God, my Holy One, you who are eternal—
    surely you do not plan to wipe us out?
O Lord, our Rock, you have sent these Babylonians to correct us,

to punish us for our many sins.

13 But you are pure and cannot stand the sight of evil.

  Will you wink at their treachery?

Should you be silent while the wicked

  swallow up people more righteous than they?

14 Are we only fish to be caught and killed?

  Are we only sea creatures that have no leader?

15 Must we be strung up on their hooks

  and caught in their nets while they rejoice and celebrate?

16 Then they will worship their nets

  and burn incense in front of them.

"These nets are the gods who have made us rich!"

  they will claim.

17 Will you let them get away with this forever?

  Will they succeed forever in their heartless conquests?

Habakkuk 2 New Living Translation (NLT)[††]

1 I will climb up to my watchtower

[††] https://www.biblegateway.com/passage/?search=Habakkuk+1-3&version=NLT

and stand at my guardpost.
There I will wait to see what the Lord says
    and how he will answer my complaint.

The Lord's Second Reply
2 Then the Lord said to me,
"Write my answer plainly on tablets,
    so that a runner can carry the correct message to others.
3 This vision is for a future time.
    It describes the end, and it will be fulfilled.
If it seems slow in coming, wait patiently,
    for it will surely take place.
    It will not be delayed.
4 "Look at the proud!
    They trust in themselves, and their lives are crooked.
    But the righteous will live by their faithfulness to God.
5 Wealth is treacherous,
    and the arrogant are never at rest.
They open their mouths as wide as the grave,
    and like death, they are never satisfied.
In their greed they have gathered up many nations

and swallowed many peoples.
6 "But soon their captives will taunt them.
    They will mock them, saying,
'What sorrow awaits you thieves!
    Now you will get what you deserve!
You've become rich by extortion,
    but how much longer can this go on?'
7 Suddenly, your debtors will take action.
    They will turn on you and take all you have,
    while you stand trembling and helpless.
8 Because you have plundered many nations,
    now all the survivors will plunder you.
You committed murder throughout the countryside
    and filled the towns with violence.
9 "What sorrow awaits you who build big houses
    with money gained dishonestly!
You believe your wealth will buy security,
    putting your family's nest beyond the reach of danger.
10 But by the murders you committed,
    you have shamed your name and forfeited your lives.
11 The very stones in the walls cry out against you,

and the beams in the ceilings echo the complaint.

12 "What sorrow awaits you who build cities
  with money gained through murder and corruption!

13 Has not the Lord of Heaven's Armies promised
  that the wealth of nations will turn to ashes?

They work so hard,
  but all in vain!

14 For as the waters fill the sea,
  the earth will be filled with an awareness
  of the glory of the Lord.

15 "What sorrow awaits you who make your neighbors drunk!
  You force your cup on them
  so you can gloat over their shameful nakedness.

16 But soon it will be your turn to be disgraced.
  Come, drink and be exposed!

Drink from the cup of the Lord's judgment,
  and all your glory will be turned to shame.

17 You cut down the forests of Lebanon.
  Now you will be cut down.

You destroyed the wild animals,
  so now their terror will be yours.

You committed murder throughout the countryside
    and filled the towns with violence.
18 "What good is an idol carved by man,
    or a cast image that deceives you?
How foolish to trust in your own creation—
    a god that can't even talk!
19 What sorrow awaits you who say to wooden idols,
    'Wake up and save us!'
To speechless stone images you say,
    'Rise up and teach us!'
    Can an idol tell you what to do?
They may be overlaid with gold and silver,
    but they are lifeless inside.
20 But the Lord is in his holy Temple.
    Let all the earth be silent before him."

Habakkuk 3 New International Version (NIV)[‡‡]
Habakkuk's Prayer (NIV)
[1] A prayer of Habakkuk the prophet. On *shigionoth*.

[‡‡] https://www.biblegateway.com/passage/?search=Habakkuk+1-3&version=NIV

²Lord, I have heard of your fame;
 I stand in awe of your deeds, Lord.
Repeat them in our day,
 in our time make them known;
 in wrath remember mercy.
³God came from Teman,
 the Holy One from Mount Paran.

           Selah

His glory covered the heavens
 and his praise filled the earth.
⁴His splendor was like the sunrise;
 rays flashed from his hand,
 where his power was hidden.
⁵Plague went before him;
 pestilence followed his steps.
⁶He stood, and shook the earth;
 he looked, and made the nations tremble.
The ancient mountains crumbled
 and the age-old hills collapsed—
 but he marches on forever.
⁷I saw the tents of Cushan in distress,

the dwellings of Midian in anguish.
[8] Were you angry with the rivers, Lord?
    Was your wrath against the streams?
Did you rage against the sea
    when you rode your horses
    and your chariots to victory?
[9] You uncovered your bow,
    you called for many arrows.

                               Selah

You split the earth with rivers;
[10] the mountains saw you and writhed.
Torrents of water swept by;
    the deep roared
    and lifted its waves on high.
[11] Sun and moon stood still in the heavens
    at the glint of your flying arrows,
    at the lightning of your flashing spear.
[12] In wrath you strode through the earth
    and in anger you threshed the nations.
[13] You came out to deliver your people,
    to save your anointed one.

You crushed the leader of the land of wickedness,
    you stripped him from head to foot.

                          Selah

[14] With his own spear you pierced his head
    when his warriors stormed out to scatter us,
gloating as though about to devour
    the wretched who were in hiding.
[15] You trampled the sea with your horses,
    churning the great waters.
[16] I heard and my heart pounded,
    my lips quivered at the sound;
decay crept into my bones,
    and my legs trembled.
Yet I will wait patiently for the day of calamity
    to come on the nation invading us.
[17] Though the fig tree does not bud
    and there are no grapes on the vines,
though the olive crop fails
    and the fields produce no food,
though there are no sheep in the pen
    and no cattle in the stalls,

[18] yet I will rejoice in the Lord,
     I will be joyful in God my Savior.
[19] The Sovereign Lord is my strength;
     he makes my feet like the feet of a deer,
     he enables me to tread on the heights.
For the director of music. On my stringed instruments.

Appendix 2: Study Guide

SOME OF US must look long and hard to find our biblical type. Are you spiritually Habakkuk? Are you obsessed with injustice? Do tough questions come easily to you?

The book of Habakkuk reminds us that we cannot stay stuck in the fist-shaking—after the wrestle, we must be willing to listen and move on.

Read the book of Habakkuk in the Bible (see Appendix 1). Reread the meditations here. Stop and pray. Stop and pray again.

Next, you'll write your own meditations. Allow time for each exercise. Linger.

First: what is your complaint? Do you have more than one complaint? What injustice affects you personally and deeply? What does it look like? What images come to mind? What honesty can you share?

Second: what are you hearing or seeing in response?

Third: where is the awe in your life? Let yourself be inspired. Write your beautiful prayer.

Gratitudes

SOME DEBTS CAN only be paid forward. Because of the amazing people God placed in my life, I have this book to offer you, dear reader.

Long after we're grown, it still takes a village, doesn't it? Here's my village.

I thank my Friday Friends small group: you were at your best when I was at my worst, when I was trying to make meaning out of a life-changing health crisis. Kind thanks to each of you: Dot Cook, Nora Gardner, Marsha Geissinger, Helene Huggett, Betsy McNamara, Karen Quinn, Deborah Simmons, Vivienne Spahn, Patti Stone, Nancy Waldron, and Peggy Young. You are indeed prayer warriors who could pray anyone through the trouble.

I thank the early readers of this manuscript: Helene Huggett, Dena Kotsores, Norma Lyon. You were brave—very brave—to take on such a task, and for that, my deep thanks.

For the tenacity to take this manuscript and give it visual appeal, I thank you, Amanda Robbins.

Kind thanks to Alan Ahlgrim, Brett Foster and Russ Parker: your thoughtful endorsements of my work meant so much to me.

Thank you, my dear friend Karen Quinn for sharing your exquisite photography skills as evidenced by your author photo.

I thank the Taos Summer Writer's Conference (summer of 2014) for its directional assistance (Jane von Mehren) as I sought to bring this project into publication. A very supportive place, indeed. A special shout out to Debra Monroe: your overall encouragement of my essay writing filled me beyond words.

I've met some unforgettable doctors over the years. Chief among them, I must thank my rehabilitation physician, Dr. Gouri Chaudhuri, at Marianjoy Medical Group in Wheaton, Illinois. Dr. Chaudhuri, you will never know how much your counsel meant to me. How eloquently you've brought me along.

Many churches and ministries over the years accompanied me on this path. My home base Rocky Mountain Christian Church in Niwot, Colorado, is one such place. Thanks, too, to the healing prayer teams and prophetic word teams at Resurrection Fellowship Church in Loveland, Colorado.

To my family—mother Natalie, father Frank, brother Larry, and sister Suzanne—my kind thanks.

To my son Ted—I am so grateful to have a son like you. And one final note of clarification about this collection that pertains to you alone: these *are* your mother's meditations.

A Note About The Author

Christine Bodine has been writing creatively for many years. Educated as a lawyer and librarian, she has worked in library, research, and educational settings throughout her career, often with writing-related roles. She received her MFA in poetry at Queens University of Charlotte, in Charlotte, North Carolina. Her chapbook *Souvenirs of Myself* was published in 2012. Having lived most of her adult life in Wheaton, Illinois, she wrote this book after her move to Colorado, where she lives today.

Made in the USA
Charleston, SC
04 November 2015